LIZ CARTER

ADVENT TREASURE

25 SHORT REFLECTIONS OF HOPE

To see more of Liz's writing and keep informed of future projects visit

greatadventure.carterclan.me.uk

Twitter: @LizCarterWriter
Facebook: @GreatAdventureLiz
Instagram: greatadventureliz

*We long for a star
when we are messes of uncertainty,
when we scream inside
through doubt-filled days
and nights of anxious ambiguity
when the world is crowded with horror
and we are cowered with unease*

*A star of wonder in velvet skies
wrapped up in untamed radiance
A star of wonder in our jagged lives
lifts up our eyes
burns through our cries
and we soar through your heights.*

Introduction

When advent approaches so many of us long to take time to reflect on verses of Scripture and think deeply about how we can further pursue God in a season often wrought with weariness, busyness and the struggles of life. We have good intentions, but then find it difficult to take the time to dig into long reflections or great chunks of Scripture.

This little book is for all who are weary, and need something quick and bite-sized, yet full of hope, reflections that will restore, comfort and inspire. Each day of advent is just one page with a short extract of poetry, a short Bible passage, quick reflection and a prayer.

As someone who is chronically ill, and often sicker through winter, I hope to express something of the treasure we can burrow into in this time of year as we journey through a time of waiting where 'creation groans' and our groans are often too deep for words, into the glorious hope that we look to as we ponder the mystery of the Incarnation.

May you know the joy of Christmas breaking through your darkness and discover the hope to which you have been called as you think on these words over the next month.

December 1

Ruach dances over unshaped deeps
breathless in expectancy
as the image of the invisible
composes a divine song

Read Genesis 1:1-5

Now the earth was formless and empty, darkness was over the surface of the deep, and the Spirit of God was hovering over the waters. (v2)

Reflect

Sometimes it feels as though the shadows of our lives are too deep. We are struggling with something; whether physical or mental ill health, or grieving, financial issues or the pain of unanswered prayer, we live under the burden of disappointment and loss, and sometimes we wonder where God is and where light is.

At the beginning of this advent season, we pause to reflect for a moment on the beginning of all ages, where the Spirit of God waited, brooding over the formless deeps, the earth shrouded in darkness as it waited itself for creation to bring it bursting into life. And then came the words that would shatter darkness and resound through the great epochs of time to come: *Let there be light.* And there was light, and that light flooded the earth and blazed through history, flooding all the darkest corners in our lives. The Spirit of God is waiting with us, too, when we cannot see through the murk ahead, dancing through our great ravines of despair, holding us close and sparking hope when hope seems lost. The Spirit reminds us that shadows do not exist without light, and so our long wait echoes with the ancient melody of hope.

Pray

Spirit of God, will you wait with me in my formless voids, hovering over my dark places when I live under pain? Flood me with light once again as you do your work of comforting and healing in me, reminding me of the hope to which I am called.

December 2

The waiting room is shrouded in darkness
no sign of light, yet
of what is to come…
just shadows in corners

Read John 1:1-14

In the beginning was the Word, and the Word was with God, and the Word was God… In him was life, and that life was the light of all mankind. The light shines in the darkness, and the darkness has not overcome it. (v1, 4-5)

Reflect

Waiting rooms can be a drain. I spend a lot of time sitting in waiting rooms, wishing the time away and seething with frustration. It's so easy to approach waiting for anything in life this way, especially if we have been waiting through years.

But what if the waiting time could be a time of light, even when the wait is tinged with darkness? What if the very wait itself is a place we can encounter God within our pain? Scripture speaks so clearly of a God who is found right in the centre of all we are facing, a God who waits with us. From the beginning Jesus spoke his words over creation and shone his light through the darkness, and although it sometimes feels as if the darkness creeps too far through our lives, we know that the darkness never has, and never will, overcome this light of life, the light that sustains and upholds. Think about how the tiniest flicker of light overcomes the darkness around it, however small an area of it – it breaks up shadows and tears apart the gloom.

When we are waiting, whether weary in waiting rooms or despondent in praying rooms, let's take hold of this incredible truth: The light always shines. The light always overcomes.

Pray

Thank you, Jesus, that your light shines through our waiting times, and your truth breaks through all of our darkness. Help me to catch a glimpse of this truth today.

December 3

Waiting with bated breath, waiting forwardly –
in this waiting room
tendrils of hope sneak in and wrap around
foretelling an enticing truth

Read Romans 15:5-13
May the God of hope fill you with all joy and peace as you trust in him, so that you may overflow with hope by the power of the Holy Spirit. (v13)

Reflect
This passage is about a promise. A promise God gave to us all, that Jesus would be a light for all nations, and it's in Jesus every person can find their hope. *Hope* and *promise* are not always easy words to hear, when we are waiting in darkness. We may feel we have hoped for good things in the past, but have not seen these hopes fulfilled. We may have read many of the promises of God in Scripture, and yet feel uncertain about how these promises have played out in our lives.

Hope can come in great big bursts, but it can also sneak into corners in tiny specks of light, weaving its peace through our anxiety and its anticipation through our despair. Sometimes we spend too long worrying about the big prayers that seem unanswered and forget to search for God's work in the small things, and to catch hold of the tendrils of hope that wrap around us when we make a decision to look towards God and trust in his promises. The word 'waiting' in Scripture is often translated as something close to 'waiting with hope'. Today let us recognise that our heavy wait can be imbued with the anticipation of enticing truth and the fulfilment of promises from the God who never fails.

Pray
Father, help us to trust in your promises, even when we cannot see through the darkness of our lives. Fill us to overflowing with the hope that sustains and lifts us up, and draw us into great anticipation.

December 4

A spark in the dark
an anticipation of the exhilaration
of our adoration
of glory wrapped in dust

Read Philippians 2:1-11

Who, being in very nature God, did not consider equality with God something to be used to his own advantage; rather, he made himself nothing… being made in human likeness. (v6-7)

Reflect

I remember my son, when he was small, toddling up to my husband when he was preaching and lifting his arms up for a 'carry.' He had confidence in his rights as a loved child.

Jesus gave up his rights as a child of his Father, emptying himself out of glory. I am in awe at his humility, and wonder at the pain he must have endured, leaving behind his royalty and landing in our mess. He couldn't even ask his Father for a hug anymore.

As you read the words of this passage today, allow the Holy Spirit to spark a sense of anticipation in you – an anticipation of what you know will, one day, become reality for you, because of Jesus' willingness to lay himself aside. The anticipation of adoring him, of being set free from the shackles of sin and the burden of pain, because Jesus is *Immanuel,* God with us, now raised and exalted to the highest place. Because he left glory and landed in dust, we can run right up to the Father and say 'Up, Daddy!' And we will be lifted up into everlasting arms, held close and comforted.

Because Jesus did not cling to his heavenly status, we can wait through our own suffering with great hope and anticipation for the glorious day when every knee will bow and every tongue confess that Jesus Christ is Lord.

Pray

Jesus, I praise you that you left your rightful place and came to earth so that I can be set free. I am amazed at your great love, and so I bow to you and confess that you are Lord.

December 5

Our wait so cold as stone, yet draped in breathless hope.
In churning restlessness and aching brokenness
a star still blazes bright,
further up and further in, we wait for dawning light.

Read Luke 2:22-40
Now there was a man in Jerusalem called Simeon, who was righteous and devout. He was waiting for the consolation of Israel, and the Holy Spirit was on him. (v25)

Reflect
Life can be full of a churning sense of restlessness. As I write this in the midst of the second wave of the pandemic, the restlessness is evident all around as people struggle with fear, loneliness, sickness, worry and grief. The world seems off kilter somehow, as if something has knocked it off balance, and we can't imagine how and when things will be right. We know deep down that things have never been right, that even before all of this we lived in brokenness. This has merely brought to light some of the injustices endemic in society – poverty, inequality, racism and ableism, and more. We are a people simmering with great unease, and we just want to go home. We just want to feel safe.

I love this story today because both Simeon and Anna were waiting through years for their consolation, for the Messiah to come. They were waiting in restless times, in broken society, and yet they clung with all their might to the hope they were waiting for. Their wait was never hopeless, and they did not fall into despondency; instead, they allowed the Holy Spirit to work within them, to point them towards that which they knew, deep down, would be reality. We, too, can be imbued with this hope when we wait in our own churning restlessness and aching brokenness.

Pray
Father, as we wait for your consolation through our own struggle, may we be shrouded in the soothing power of your Spirit, and know you will come once more and triumph over injustice.

December 6

Waiting for love to come down –
Impossible love. Inexplicable love. Incomprehensible love.
Love that holds us where we are
and contains all we are

Read Ephesians 3:14-20

And I pray that you, being rooted and established in love, may have power… to grasp how wide and long and high and deep is the love of Christ…' (v17-18)

Reflect

Love came down at Christmas, goes the poem by Christina Rosetti. Divine love is inexplicable, it's incomprehensible, it's inexpressible, but it is something that we know we need more of. Come on a journey with me for a few moments today, taking time over these words, allowing God to minister his love to you in a new way:

Plunge into the glorious riches of God – too exquisite to behold, and be restored with power through the Spirit in your deepest soul. Put your roots ever deeper into the love that never gives up on you, and grasp how wide and long and high and deep, how immense and immeasurable and boundless and profound, how sweeping and towering and soaring and unfathomable is the love of our Lord Jesus. Be drowned in this love that passes all knowledge and eclipses all learning, so that you may be filled to bursting with all the fullness of God. Now to God who is able to do immeasurably, boundlessly, limitlessly more than all you could ever ask, and all you could ever imagine, according to his power at work within you, everywhere you go and everything you do, to God be the honour, the praise, the acclaim and the exaltation, and in Christ Jesus throughout all generations, through history, stretching back and forth to eternity.

Pray

Father, I stand amazed at your incomparable love. Sweep me further up and draw me further in as I worship you today.

December 7

Love that fires us
and inspires us
love that shimmers through our darkness
waiting
for love to come down

Read Isaiah 9:1-7

The people walking in darkness have seen a great light; on those living in the land of deep darkness a light has dawned. (v2)

Reflect

I remember one moment as a youngster when the truth of the gospel came crashing over me anew. It was during a Christmas event, where we were out on the streets with proper old-fashioned flaming torches (health and safety didn't exist in the 80s, evidently), singing Christmas carols and giving out mince pies. As we stood outside a row of shops someone read this Bible passage and it felt as though gold was rushing through my veins, as I heard the ancient words of Isaiah talking about a saviour from Galilee. My burning torch seemed to glow brighter through the murky gloom of a winter evening as I realised that we, also, were the people living in darkness who had seen a great light. I remember being so struck by how the land around me was still a place of deep darkness, and a new craving in me for God's light to dawn and for people to be set free. And when verses 6 and 7 were read out I was stunned by their power and truth, truth that keeps lighting up all the dark corners, truth that this Prince of Peace, this Wonderful Counsellor, this Mighty God, this Everlasting Father did indeed become one of us, born into our aching world.

Be lifted by these words today as you think on them, asking the Spirit to breathe whispers of peace on earth and endless joy.

Pray

Thank you, Jesus, that your light has dawned on us and ignites hope in us. Thank you that you breathed these words so long ago, knowing that they would thrill and sustain through all of history.

December 8

A weary world watching,
waiting;
yearning expectancy for whispers of eternity
a flicker of light
explodes in reflections of a million starbursts

Read Luke 1:26-38

The angel answered, 'The Holy Spirit will come on you, and the power of the Most High will overshadow you. So the holy one to be born will be called the Son of God. (v35)

Reflect

Last year I bought a new Christmas tree to put in my bay window – it's one of those that resemble a winter tree, devoid of leaves, but studded with tiny fairy lights on each branch. Before we decorated it further I switched the main light off and the tree lights on, and stood back, dazzled by the reflection of the lights in the window. It was as if there was suddenly an infinity of lights in unfathomable depths, and the further I gazed into the window the more of the lights I could see, almost dancing in their millions. I stood and thought about how one tiny light can have such a startling and powerful effect.

It reminded me of how Jesus was born from such humble beginnings, how one young woman who wanted to obey the God she loved would be someone who changed history. In a weary world, a society under oppression, from a culture where she knew she would be judged and found wanting, Mary listened for whispers of eternity and responded. A flicker of light became a conflagration of hope, a million stars of utter joy, as the Saviour of the world was conceived by the power of the Holy Spirit.

Pray

God of light, may I reflect your love in a million different directions as the incomprehensible power of it roots deep down inside me. May I listen for your whispers of eternity, even when I am weary and waiting, and hear the peace of your call upon me.

December 9

Somewhere bells are ringing, resounding through our pain
somewhere love is flinging our misery far away.
Peals of peace rip through the mist –
hear their alluring call, and wait for joy to fall.

Read Luke 1:39-56
'As soon as the sound of your greeting reached my ears, the baby in my womb leaped for joy. Blessed is she who has believed that the Lord would fulfil his promises to her!' (v44-45)

Reflect
Elizabeth had struggled greatly through life, in a world hostile to those women who could not bear children. Yet she saw the promises of God play out when she bore a son at an impossible age, and heard the whisper of God through her years of pain.
Many of us don't seem to see the big answers, the big miracles, so how do we respond to the promises of God and the whispers of the Spirit in our own lives? For me, on some days it's just that small reminder of God's ultimate hope that carries me through. I'm clinging on by my fingertips, uncertain and all my courage leaking away, but then I remember that it is God who is holding on to me, and I can let go a while, be bathed in his comfort as he tends my wounds. Perhaps you, today, need that reminder that God is simply here, inside your misery with you, and is tending you so very gently. God hears your cry; he hears the pain of infertility, or the pain of loss, or the pain of sickness, and he feels it, too. May you know his great peace ripping through your mist, and sense his alluring call to your spirit, so that you leap for joy from the darkest places, as John leapt for joy at the presence of the one he knew had come to heal and save.

Pray
Lord, sometimes my misery is too big for me, and I need you to hold me a while. Thank you that you call to me with a gentle whisper, and that your light shatters my gloom. Call to me today, Lord, and may my spirit leap for joy in your great hope.

December 10

They say the darkest hours lurk before dawn
soupy blackness
a struggle of dejection and hope
wrestling through hours, as I wait

Read Isaiah 52:7-10

Burst into songs of joy together, you ruins of Jerusalem, for the Lord has comforted his people, he has redeemed Jerusalem. (v9)

Reflect

Sometimes our lives feel as though they have fallen into ruin, as if there is no possibility of restoration, as if the darkness is too soupy and the ruins too fragmented. But this passage of Scripture reminds us today that ruins can burst into songs of joy, that our shattered lives can be restored, that the good news of the gospel overcomes all the wreckage that lies around us. It reminds us that God's plan for us is peace and salvation, and his love brings immense joy found nowhere else. It reminds us that hope will triumph over dejection, and our God reigns over it all.

One of the most powerful images I have seen over the past couple of years is the picture of the golden cross in the smoking ruins of Notre Dame, the cross still standing triumphant and captivating through the devastation. It's such a potent picture of the power of the cross, still glowing bright through the ravages of time and the wreckage in our lives, because Jesus has conquered the power of sin and death, and this same power lives in us. Today, reflect for a while on this image, as you pray these words:

Pray

You shine in ruins
your cross a never-changing symbol
of a never-changing love.
May the ruins come to life again –
may the waste places shout for joy,
and the desolate, long-forgotten places praise your name.

December 11

I search for the tiniest flame of hope
the gloom is leaden with thick despair
but I see wisps of shadows in corners
flickerings of daybreak; echoes of the dawn sky

Read Luke 1:57-80

By the tender mercy of our God, the dawn from on high will break upon us, to give light to those who sit in darkness and in the shadow of death, to guide our feet into the way of peace. (v78-79, NRSV)

Reflect

I remember travelling down to Dover through the night to catch the early morning ferry. I watched as the inky blackness morphed slowly into the dawn, stunned at the glory of it. At first, though, only very slightly perceptible grey lines slashed through the sky, hardly different from the pitch black all around. I watched as the grey slowly lightened and turned to muted corals and indigos, and then it was as if an artist began to paint vibrant colours across the canvas of the skies, and dawn arrived in all its splendour.

When we are waiting for the dawn, it can seem to take a long time to arrive. For a while, we might not be able to perceive anything but darkness, and then only the odd streak of grey, hardly cause for an outbreak of joy. But it's the knowledge that the dawn will come and the colours will blaze that keeps us waiting with hope.

Zechariah and Elizabeth caught hold of a flame of hope as their story of sadness and despair was shattered by God's promise. Zechariah's song is one of awed praise as he perceives the colours of dawn exploding into their lives in breathtaking majesty. We see echoes of this when we look to the waking skies and remember God's glorious dawn breaking out of history and upon us.

Pray

Jesus, your voice is the dawn from on high breaking over us, and your love is the explosion of colour over our waiting skies. May we perceive your glorious dawn breaking into this day.

December 12

The days are too long as we wait for a song
and search for horizons of hope
We wait in our dreams and we wait with our tears
as you call to the wilds in our souls.

Read Isaiah 11:1-10

In that day the Root of Jesse will stand as a banner for the peoples; the nations will rally to him, and his resting-place will be glorious. (v10)

Reflect

What is your favourite resting-place? Where do you go when you need to recuperate, to get restored? I love to go near water, whether the sea, lakes or rivers, or even a bubbling stream. There is something calming about the sound of the water. Great wide-open beaches are my favourite places, where the skies meet the wildness of the ocean and the Creator's hand is so evident.

For many of us, though, a place is not enough. We can lie on a beach and feel rested, but our soul can still be seething with unease. We can plant our gardens and be restored, but our minds can still be broken into pieces. We all crave a greater resting-place, a place where our tears will be dried up, where we will be whole in every way. Today's passage reminds us that Jesus, in the line of David, son of Jesse, was prophesied about from ancient times as a lifter of the needy and a lover of righteousness, but also as a bringer of a kingdom of wholeness where the wolf will lie with the lamb and the calf with the lion, where there will be no more destruction, and where there will be glorious rest. And as we wait with our own tears, we are encouraged by these great word-pictures of what will come, and catch hold of the edges of this great and glorious truth: God come down to us.

Pray

God, be my resting-place today within the storms that I face. Be the place I go to for peace, and the rock that I cling to when the world is hostile. Thank you that you became incarnate for me.

December 13

The nights are too dark as we wait for a spark
and yearn for a day of delight
We wait in our pain and we wait in our chains
for your glory to burst through the night.

Read Revelation 21:1-6

He will wipe every tear from their eyes. There will be no more death or mourning or crying or pain, for the old order of things has passed away. He who was seated on the throne said, "I am making everything new!" (v4-5)

Reflect

Yesterday we reflected on our need for a resting-place for our souls as well as our bodies. But it's not only rest that we need – it's joy, as well. It's delight, excitement and adventure we long for, because we know that we are made for joy.

Advent is a season of preparation, not just for the celebration of Jesus' birth but for preparing ourselves for when Jesus will return and renew the earth. All the emptiness and yearning in us will be filled and fulfilled, and all the waiting come to a glorious close as glory bursts through the night. All our pain will be taken away, all our tears will be dried up and our mourning be eased at last. Joy will break through and flood our weary souls, joy that will be uncontained and wild, joy so vivid and vibrant that we will be unable to keep it in. As Jesus comes and makes everything new, we will be made new, too, our bodies and our minds, the depths of our souls, all renewed and re-created into the splendour of who we were always created to be.

But we don't have this hope only as something to cling to for the future. It's a hope that bursts into our lives now as we take hold of this truth, as we abandon ourselves in worship, as our souls respond to the greatest delight of God's uncontainable love.

Pray

Jesus, I choose to worship you through all of my struggles. Renew me today, and flood me with a new sense of joy as I look to you.

December 14

Waiting for a sight of a pinprick of light
to ignite a silent night.
We lift our tired eyes as our depths burst out in cries
of hope in flickers of colour – the waiting almost over.

Read Isaiah 35

They will enter Zion with singing; everlasting joy will crown their heads. Gladness and joy will overtake them, and sorrow and sighing will flee away. (v10)

Reflect

I often feel very feeble. Some days my breathing is so bad I can barely make it up the stairs (some days I can't make it down them!) My body is clothed in weakness, and life can seem incredibly tiring. I wonder if you're feeling a little like that too – if not physically, perhaps you feel like you are mentally unable to cope, and simply tired of it all.

You're so exhausted in your wait. Yet this passage speaks of hope that doesn't only sustain but fires with great anticipation. The desert and the parched land will be glad. The wilderness you are in will be a place of blossoming, a place where your God will strengthen your feeble hands and steady your shaking knees. God is saying to you today, 'Be strong, do not fear – your God will come.'

And your God has come. Your God has come with justice and compassion, with righteousness and salvation. Your God has come to heal and to save, to bring water gushing through your desert places. Today, may you enter Zion with singing and catch a glimpse of what it means for everlasting joy to crown your weary head. May your sorrow and sighing flee far away as you remember what this advent wait is for.

Pray

Father, strengthen my feeble hands today, steady my shaky knees. May I walk on the way of holiness as you draw me closer to you, and as I sigh with my sorrow may I know a shower of your joy.

December 15

The bells ring out with praise
the mystery of Immanuel
draws our weary gaze
and rays of glorious light ignite our darkest night

Read Colossians 1:15-23

The Son is the image of the invisible God, the firstborn over all creation. For in him all things were created: things in heaven and on earth, visible and invisible, whether thrones or powers or rulers or authorities; all things have been created through him and for him. (v15-16)

Reflect

The mystery of Immanuel draws our weary gaze.

Take a few moments today to wrap yourself in this mystery as you plunge into these profound words of Scripture. Walk out deeper into this ocean of grace, into these glorious truths: Jesus, God incarnate, was there at the start of the ages, crafting galaxies and singing over creation. The day was born with a shout of exultation, and the moon and stars bowed in elation, to Immanuel. God with us. Jesus, God incarnate, by whom all things were created, was born in poverty and darkness, turning on its head the prevailing narrative of a world that loves success and honour. Jesus, Immanuel, for whom all things were created, loved us so much that he was born in dishonour and died in disgrace, loved us so much that he conquered death so that we would be set free from its insidious power. Jesus, God incarnate, is with us today in the power and joy of the Spirit, wrapping up our weariness and igniting our darkness.

Allow your weary gaze to be drawn to Immanuel today.

Pray

Ignite our darkness, O Lord of light, O image of the invisible, Creator of all things. Draw our weary gaze to you and bring forth our praise to you, as we drown in the mystery of love incomprehensible.

December 16

Frozen in time so long now
a journey of weary darkness
but the waiting is almost over
a dawn of something like hope

Read Micah 5:1-4

But you, Bethlehem Ephrathah, though you are small among the clans of Judah, out of you will come for me one who will be ruler over Israel, whose origins are from of old, from ancient times. (v2)

Reflect

For many of us, this pandemic year has seemed frozen in time, as if we are trapped in its walls, unable to leave and unable to break out. We look to the end of it for hope, wishing the days away and wondering if hibernating through the winter might be a good plan. Sometimes our lives seem like this, suspended in time, waiting for better days and brighter sunshine. Time does not heal us, but instead imposes more scars on us as our waits stretch longer.

But Christmas is a message of hope through the scars of time because its origins are from eternity, from ancient times, from the very throne of God. I love that God always uses the weak things of the world to shame the strong. Instead of being born in state, in a great palace of a great city, Jesus was born in a small town, a nothing place, a place that wasn't noted for its importance. Jesus was born in humility so that he could bring his saving grace crashing through lives that don't look like perfection, that feel frozen in time because they hurt too much. Today, be comforted by Jesus, of ancient origins and yet born into humble beginnings on earth, knowing that your time is contained in God's great epochs of time that have passed and will come to pass.

Pray

Break into my frozen winter, O Lord my God. Rend my time with your eternal love, breathing your ancient whispers through the ragged canyons of my soul, and drawing me into hope.

December 17

Now the sky explodes in golden evanescence
hope streaks the great canvas
as glorious sunrise sweeps through the pain in me
and joy breaks in at last.

Read Psalm 8

When I consider your heavens, the work of your fingers, the moon and the stars which you have set in place, what is mankind that you are mindful of them, human beings that you care for them? (v3-4)

Reflect

Through the long days of winter I often miss the open skies and velvet nights of summer, where stars seem closer and galaxies shout loud over the glorious canvas. I long for the morning to come, for the springtime with its explosion of life and colour, but I am stuck in my sick-bed once again, waiting through winter.

Yet that is the very time when it is good to reflect upon the mystery of the love and grace of God, and to gaze upon his creativity. The writer of this Psalm captures a longing in all of us; a longing to know and to be known, to understand how and why God would love us, to take hold of this love and express it in praise. As the writer contemplates the sweep of the heavens, he is stunned and awed by the Creator's love for humanity.

You are known by the God who crafted the stars. But more than that; you are passionately loved and you are pursued by this God. Look to the skies tonight, through the winter gloom, and search for the glory beyond understanding.

Be still in God's presence now for a few moments and bathe in this truth: You are loved by the one who wrote the heights and depths of space.

Pray

Father God, creator of life, thank you that you love me. Thank you for your astonishing craftsmanship. As I wait through this long winter, be present with me, folding me tight in everlasting arms.

December 18

Torn up with waiting, longing for more
searching in long-forgotten spaces
for long hoped-for traces
of light in dark places

Read Isaiah 61
They will rebuild the ancient ruins and restore the places long devastated; they will renew the ruined cities that have been devastated for generations. (v4)

Reflect
Do you sometimes feel as though your life has fallen into ruins, as if the landscape of your life lies devastated as you wait for more?
These verses are part of a longer section in the book of Isaiah concentrating on prophecies about a messianic Saviour, and these are the words Jesus claims for his own ministry right at the start (Luke 4:16-21) These extraordinary words hold at the heart an astounding truth, and that truth abounds through the *insteads*.
In the *insteads* we find a radical turnaround of brokenness, mourning and despair, and when we begin to live in the *instead* world of God's kingdom, we begin to rebuild the ancient ruins in our life, to restore long devastated wild places in the depths of us. When we embrace the *instead*, our chains are shattered into pieces and we find ourselves free, with no bars across our lives.
When you find yourself back in your ancient ruins, caged within the words that hold you captive and the untruths that shadow your soul, find yourself emancipated by God's great *insteads*. Find yourself standing high on restored walls and dressed in praise, as you take your eyes off your own story and find yourself in the greater story of who God is.

Pray
Father, I thank you that you are a God of *insteads*, a God who turns devastation into renewal. Today will you restore my ruins, transforming my ashes into a crown of beauty, my mourning into the oil of joy and my despair into a garment of praise.

December 19

T'was the night before Christmas,
and all through our souls
was a sigh full of yearning
through time's aching toll

Read Psalm 63:1-8

You, God, are my God, earnestly I seek you; I thirst for you, my whole being longs for you, in a dry and parched land where there is no water. (v1)

Reflect

It's long been a tradition in our house to read the poem 'T'was the Night Before Christmas' by Clement Clarke Moore together on Christmas Eve. The sense of anticipation and longing that marches through the poem is tangible in the room, and the joy of the words awakens a need for delight and adventure, for excitement and joy. Even though my children are now young adults, they still like to listen to my husband read it out.

There is a sense of yearning at the centre of all of us as human beings. David captures it here in this passage as he grieves over his painful present, isolated in the desert, far from home and far from God. He reminds himself of how God's love is better than life, how God satisfies his soul like no other. He turns his sorrow into worship and sings out his praise and his intention to remember God's work through the watches of the night.

I wonder if you are feeling a bit like David today. Perhaps you are isolated and lonely, wandering through the wilderness, uncertain about the future. As you turn to God once again through your pain, may you be filled with a sense of yearning that bursts into anticipation, as your whole being is filled with a love that is better than life and more satisfying than the richest of food.

Pray

Lord, my inmost being longs for you, like a dry and weary land longs for water. Hear my sigh of yearning and satisfy my longing, O God, and cascade your love into the deepest parts of me.

December 20

Eyes wide with wonder, breathless with hope
a song resounds through the sweep of the night
the long wait drawing to a close
in an explosion of saving light

Read Luke 2:8-20

Suddenly a great company of the heavenly host appeared with the angel, praising God and saying, 'Glory to God in the highest heaven, and on earth peace to those on whom his favour rests.' (v13-14)

Reflect

Imagine, for a moment, that you are out in the fields with the other shepherds. The night is dark, the skies are studded with stars and silence shrouds you like a great cloud. You are weary and sleepy.

Suddenly the sky seems to change before your eyes, as if dawn is singing its morning song too early, as if a painter has thrown a riot of colours across the great canvas. You are dazzled and afraid all at once. When the angel appears, he says, 'Do not be afraid,' and you fall on your face because you cannot look on the light even though you long to sink into it, you are drawn to it and you yearn for more of it. When the heavenly host join together in a song you want to be a part of it: it is alluring and enticing, it is ancient and brand new, it calls to the wild parts of you. You know that your long wait has drawn to a close.

Today, may you catch glimpses of that blazing light as you think on these words. May you be filled to bursting with the certainty that your wait will come to an end, but that even in your waiting you can be flooded with peace beyond comprehension.

Pray

Blaze through my darkness, God enthroned in heavenly light, and draw me closer to your unconditional and uncontainable love. Fill me with anticipation and longing for more of you as I look to the skies in wonder, and hear your ancient call on me.

December 21

We wait in expectation
of our joyful liberation
from the groaning of creation
waiting to kneel in adoration

Read Romans 8:18-28

We know that the whole creation has been groaning as in the pains of childbirth right up to the present time. Not only so, but we ourselves, who have the firstfruits of the Spirit, groan inwardly as we wait eagerly for our adoption to sonship, the redemption of our bodies. (v22-23)

Reflect

We reflected yesterday on the shepherds and their experience of the saving power of God breaking into their lives. They, like many of us, must have understood the depth behind these words today: the groaning of creation, the crying out to be made whole, the mourning for restoration. And then, as they found the baby and the words of the angel became truth before them, they knelt in adoration, utterly floored by this light that so abruptly interrupted their darkness and called them further in to something new and wonderful.

Are you groaning, along with creation, for wholeness? Are you sick of bondage to decay, longing for liberation? Be reminded today of the presence of God through the Spirit who helps you in your weakness and intercedes for you in groans even deeper than your own. Be reminded that God is working for your good in all things, even through days and nights of harsh winter. As you kneel in adoration, be liberated into joy as you eagerly wait for the fullness of life God has imbued you with as his adopted child.

Pray

Father, today I offer to you my groans too deep for words. I thank you that you hear the deepest cries of my heart and that your Spirit intercedes for me. Set me free as I eagerly wait for you.

December 22

T'was the night before Christmas,
and all through our dreams
a lament full of hunger
for a love of extremes.

Read Psalm 27

One thing I ask from the Lord, this only do I seek: that I may dwell in the house of the Lord all the days of my life, to gaze on the beauty of the Lord and to seek him in his temple. (v4)

Reflect

Human love can be a wonderful thing. The love of friends and family can be sustaining and powerful, it can bring much-needed joy to our lives, it can bring fun and laughter, consolation and honesty. But it's never perfect – and if we expect perfection, we're heading for a fall. Sometimes loved ones let us down, sometimes we are abandoned and rejected. That's because human love, while a glorious mix of beauty and hope, only dimly reflects the greater and wider love of our Creator. As a parent, I have done my best to love my children, but there are times I've failed them and hurt them. Yet God's love never fails. God's love is the strength of our hearts, our light and our salvation, the antidote to the fear that seethes through our souls. God will not reject us.

God's love is so powerful because of Jesus. If Jesus had not come to earth, if he had not laid aside his majesty and got into our mess, if he had not suffered the most immense pain, we would not have a God whose love conquers all our fear and struggle. But he did. He is God incarnate, love come down, word became flesh. And at the centre of us is a longing for more of this love, a yearning to dwell in his house and to gaze on his beauty. Today, let us enter into his house with joy and gratitude.

Pray

Lord, your love never fails. Thank you that your love is stronger than death itself. Take me closer into you today, O God of hope.

December 23

The winter is past;
the rains are over and gone,
find love that is deep and love that is long
find immersive light and ageless depths
find crazy love in inexorable breadth

Read Song of Songs 2:8-13

'Arise, my darling, my beautiful one, come with me. See! The winter is past; the rains are over and gone. Flowers appear on the earth; the season of singing has come.' (v10-12)

Reflect

Winter can seem unending at times, when the days are dull and the nights are oppressive. It's difficult to see signs of spring when winter grips the land in frozen captivity. Our lives can feel like that at times, too. Sometimes we can only see the dark nights and the rain-pounded days. We close our eyes in great weariness, and ask God where he has gone.

But hope lurks on our horizons, when we look close enough, when we take hold of it with courage and tenacity, when we are strengthened by the Spirit and comforted by the love of God that holds us when we fall. This passage always speaks so clearly to me of the nature of hope, of God extending his hand to you and calling you his beloved, his beautiful one – that is who you are! Your winter is past, he whispers to you, and his whispers are songs of hope. The flowers will come, the singing will come. Just hang in there a little while longer, dear one, just keep taking hold of this truth, this gospel, this life-changing story which impacts and captivates and draws you closer to the very heart of love. Your rains will be over and gone. With two days until Christmas, allow the joy of the Christ-child to begin to break through today.

Pray

O Lord, who brings frozen winter to an end and ushers in the glory of spring, remind me today of your work in my life. May your Holy Spirit fall on me anew, and lead me into hope.

December 24

A star of wonder in velvet skies
wrapped up in untamed radiance
A star of wonder in our jagged lives
lifts up our eyes, burns through our cries
and we soar through your heights.

Read Isaiah 60

The sun will no more be your light by day, nor will the brightness of the moon shine on you, for the Lord will be your everlasting light, and your God will be your glory. (v19)

Reflect

On Christmas Eve I love to go to a candlelit carol service and soak up the great hope captured in the juxtaposition of light and darkness. But most years lately I have been confined to my bed, or sofa, or a hospital bed, caged in by my disease through lungs that don't work very well. I look at Christmas from the outside in, longing to be a part of it, sorrow swelling in my heart. This year, as we live under restrictions for Covid, many of us are feeling this sadness, as if Christmas joy has been sucked out by the darkness of disease.

Thick darkness covers the earth, Isaiah says in this passage. Darkness over all the people. The profound depths of these words always brings me to a greater awareness of the contrast of light and dark, as I look around me at the truth of this statement in our world today, at the thickness of the dark that closes in around us. But gloom turns to hope as his next words shatter apart the murk. The Lord will rise upon us. His glory will appear on us. Our dawn will be bright and so we lift up our eyes, and our days of sorrow will end. Today, may you experience untamed radiance that shatters your darkness, and as you look to the skies on Christmas Eve, lift up your eyes and see a star of wonder.

Pray

Dear Jesus, as I look with anticipation to the hope of tomorrow, shatter my darkness and rise upon me. Lift up my eyes, O Lord.

December 25

JOY IN THE MORNING

A hark the herald in a weary cave
* A midnight clear blinks through our fears*
And all ye faithful come and praise
* As a silent night is draped in light*

A bleak midwinter awakened to spring
* As shepherds hear angels from glory realms*
On Christmas night the whole world sings
* O come, O come, Immanuel*

O little town, your story resounds
* Through first nowells and merrily bells*
Through a manger away and a shining new day
* We salute the morn as the anthem swells*

O see amid our winter pain
* Amid our night where dread takes flight*
What child is this, who rests our shame
* Joy to the world in a brand-new name*

A hark the herald in our weary souls
* A midnight clear in our deepest fears*
A little town of hallowed ground
* And joy in the morning when you are here.*

Read Matthew 1:18-25

All this took place to fulfill what the Lord had said through the prophet: "The virgin will conceive and give birth to a son, and they will call him Immanuel" (which means "God with us"). (v22-23)

Reflect

We've walked a journey through waiting and wilderness, through bitterness and despair, through horizons of hope and whispers of eternity. We've given our own painful waiting to God and allowed the Holy Spirit to console us in our darkness.

And now comes the morning. Now comes the joy, the dawn breaking in great evanescence, the colours of day sweeping the skies. Now comes salvation, a promise fulfilled and the dawning of redeeming hope, the edges of a dream and the warmth of the greatest truth. Now comes the new day, a day of triumph and weeping coming to an end. The day of Immanuel, God with us.

This story of a weary cave, a baby in a manger and a midnight clear, this tale of angels and shepherds and wise ones with gifts, is a story that has stood the test of great ages of time. Its truth streams through history, through all of our past and all of our present, through all of our brokenness and all of our pain. Its truth continues to spark hope in countless lives today, as we turn back to the one who came to earth because his love is greater than we can imagine.

Take time, through the haze of tinsel and turkey, to contemplate on the beauty of this truth. Take a few moments now to thank God for his love, and the greatest gift of all.

The gift of Immanuel.

Pray

Thank you Jesus that you came down at Christmas. Thank you for your great love that broke into history in the shadow of darkness and exploded all the shards of that darkness into glorious light. Thank you that today, I can celebrate the dawn of redeeming grace, the beginning of the greatest story, the birth of hope that captivates and sustains me, just as it has for so many over the ages.

Jesus, Light of the World, lighten my darkness.

Jesus, Saviour of the World, free me from my bonds.

Jesus, Hope of the World, draw me into your inexpressible joy.

Thanks be to God for his indescribable gift!

2 Corinthians 9:15

Thank You

The poetry in this devotional is taken from my book *Treasure in Dark Places: Stories and poems of hope in the hurting* which was written in shielding through the pandemic of 2020, and is available to purchase on Amazon, Eden, Waterstones and other online stores, or can be ordered from your local Christian bookshop.

You might like my other books:

A Tale of Beauty from Ashes – A six session Bible study course based around the film *Beauty and the Beast*

Catching Contentment: How to be Holy Satisfied (IVP) – is it possible to find contentment when life hurts?

Catching Contentment: How to be Holy Satisfied – A six session Bible study course.

If you want to know more, do have a look at my website and sign up to my mailing list at:

greatadventure.carterclan.me.uk

Twitter: @LizCarterWriter
Facebook: @GreatAdventureLiz
Instagram: greatadventureliz

Many thanks and blessings,

Liz Carter

Printed in Great Britain
by Amazon

32617824R00022